TRAVEL BILBAO
ULTIMATE TRAVEL GUIDE TO BILBAO WITH ESSENTIAL TIPS ON HOW TO NAVIGATE THE CITY'S BEAUTY, MONUMENTS, AND BEACHES.

BRIAN E. SMITH

All right reserved. No part of this publication should be reproduced, distributed, or transmitted in any form or by any means, including photocopying, recording, or other electronic or mechanical methods, without the prior written permission of the publisher, except in the case of brief quotations embodied in critical reviews and certain other noncommercial uses permitted by copyright law.

Copyright@ Brian E. Smith, 2023.

TABLE OF CONTENT

CHAPTER 1
    INTRODUCTION TO BILBAO
CHAPTER 2
    STRUCTURING A PROFITABLE TRAVEL TO BILBAO
CHAPTER 3
    BEST TIME FOR TRAVELERS TO VISIT BILBAO
CHAPTER 4
    BILBAO'S ACCOMMODATION AND TRANSPORTATION OPTIONS
CHAPTER 5
    MAJOR ACTIVITIES FOR TOURISTS IN BILBAO
CHAPTER 6
    BILBAO FOODS AND DRINKS
CHAPTER 7
    BILBAO SHOPPING: THINGS YOU NEED TO KNOW
CHAPTER 8
    NIGHTLIFE IN BILBAO

CHAPTER 1

INTRODUCTION TO BILBAO

Bilbao is a city in Basque, situated in northern Spain and to the north of the Iberian Peninsula. Bilbao is a rich and vibrant city with a top-notch location to experience Iberian culture, take in the wonderful weather, or just unwind on the beach.

It is a dynamic and culturally diverse city nestled in the gorgeous Nervión River Valley. Bilbao has become a fascinating destination for tourists from all over the globe because it combined history, modernism, and breathtaking natural surroundings.

History: Bilbao, known as a modest fishing community, came into existence in the 14th century. But Bilbao underwent a tremendous shift in the late 19th and early 20th centuries as a result of the industrial revolution. Due mostly to its iron and steel industries, the city developed into a significant industrial center. The urban environment of Bilbao was formed by this era of industry, and as it expanded, landmark buildings and architectural treasures were built that are still standing today.

Modern Transformation: Bilbao witnessed a significant regeneration and reinvention in the late 20th century. Construction of the Guggenheim Museum Bilbao, a Frank Gehry-designed architectural wonder, catalyzed this shift. Since its opening in 1997, the museum has attracted tourists from all around the world. Its curved titanium facade and collection of modern art helped Bilbao become well-known worldwide, revitalizing the city's image and increasing tourism.

Bilbao's urban environment exhibits a tasteful fusion of old and new in terms of architecture and urban design. Other prominent architectural features in addition to the Guggenheim Museum are the Euskalduna Palace, an amazing convention and performing arts facility situated on the riverbank, and the Zubizuri Bridge, a beautiful white footbridge created by Santiago Calatrava.

The skyline of the city is speckled with a variety of sleek, modern buildings and historic Basque constructions, exhibiting Bilbao's architectural diversity.

Bilbao takes great pride in its Basque roots and has been able to maintain its cultural character. The Euskara language, unique to the Basque people, is one of the oldest in Europe and is extensively used in the area. Festivals, music, dancing, and gastronomic experiences are just a few of the ways the city honors its cultural heritage.

Visitors have the chance to get fully immersed in Basque culture and take part in customary activities like Basque pelota matches, energetic street festivals, and colorful local markets.

Bilbao has a wide variety of museums and galleries that feature a wide variety of creative expressions, making it a sanctuary for art connoisseurs. In addition to holding an incredible collection of modern art and presenting temporary exhibits, the Guggenheim

Museum Bilbao is a must-see. Another important organization is the Bilbao Fine Arts Museum, which has a sizable collection of works dating from the Middle Ages to the present. Additionally, the Alhóndiga Bilbao, a cultural and recreation hub situated in a former wine warehouse, offers diverse cultural events and showcases modern art.

Bilbao and Basque cuisine are famous across the globe for their high quality and distinctive tastes. The region's wealth of fresh local foods is highlighted by the city's culinary sector, which is steeped in history. Visitors may partake in the popular pintxos culture, which involves eating small dishes while sipping local wine or cider.

There are several pintxos bars along the streets of Bilbao, each serving a distinctive selection of mouthwatering snacks. Bilbao provides a gastronomic feast with everything from succulent Basque cheeses and charcuterie to freshly grilled seafood.

Natural Beauty & Outdoor Activities: Visitors may enjoy a wide variety of outdoor activities and breathtaking natural beauty because of Bilbao's strategic position between mountains and the sea. Those who like the outdoors may go on beautiful walks in the nearby mountains, such as Mount Artxanda, which provides sweeping views of the city and its lovely environs.

The Nervión River's pedestrian route, the Bilbao Riverwalk, offers a tranquil retreat from the busy city center and enables guests to take in the city's riverfront attractiveness and rich vegetation.

Bilbao is ideally situated close to the breathtaking Basque coastline for visitors looking for a seaside experience. Explore the stunning beaches, such as Playa de Ereaga in Getxo, where visitors may bask in the sun, cool off in the water, or take a leisurely walk along the promenade. A visit to the coastal communities of Bermeo and Lekeitio is particularly recommended because of their endearing fishing ports, classic architecture, and vibrant marine environment.

Bilbao is close to San Sebastian, a compelling coastal town famed for its top-notch culinary scene, stunning beaches, and lovely Old Town. Vitoria-Gasteiz, the capital of the Basque Country, is another noteworthy journey because of its ancient city center and green areas. Wine enthusiasts may make the short trip to the adjacent Rioja wine area to partake in wine tours and tastings at famous vineyards.

RELEVANT INFORMATION ABOUT BILBAO

Here are some general informational facts about Bilbao, from its history to its geography:

1. Bilbao was founded in 1300.

In its early years, the city of Bilbao was home to a community of seafarers. The "Nervión's" estuary was not far from it. The locals immediately gained widespread recognition for the manufacturing of iron and later ironworks.

On June 15, 1300, Don Diego V de Haro established the city with a municipal charter, which King Ferdinand IV of Castile subsequently validated on January 4, 1301. As soon as wool was sent to Flanders, it began to develop into a significant port and economic hub.

2. For both the city and the nation as a whole, Bilbao's port is crucial.

Bilbao's port is one of the most significant in the whole nation due to its significance. With the export of iron ore beginning in 1870, the city saw a very quick industrialization expansion. A strong Basque nationalist response resulted from the city's rapid growth, which attracted large numbers of additional Spanish workers from all around the nation.

With that, Bilbao swiftly responded to the shift in global business and expanded its services and tourism, particularly with the 1997 opening of the Guggenheim Museum.

3. Bilbao remains the biggest city in the Basque country.

A Spanish autonomous community is the Basque Country. It is in the North and well-known for having a distinctive identity—much like Catalonia, it is an area with strong separatist ambitions.

With more than 350,000 residents, Bilbao is by far the biggest city in the Basque Country, followed by Vitoria-Gasteiz, which has more than 238,000 residents. Although the Basque Country does not have a designated capital, Bilbao is ineligible since Vitoria-Gasteiz is where the Parliament is situated.

4. Bilbao is split into two halves.

The Nervión River, where Bilbao was built and is still today, divides the city. The city is divided into two sections: one is devoted to industry, and the other to trade.

The early part of the city is mostly made up of working-class areas and industry. The commercial, historic, and residential sectors are seen in the other. As a result, the city is divided between ancient and modern sections, which are connected by 9 bridges.

5. Numerous significant industries have Bilbao as support.

Despite iron and wool being the city's initial two major commercial successes, it has evolved significantly throughout time. With the fall of the steel sector in the 1970s, tourism, and services gained significant importance in the city.

Additionally, Bilbao is a significant player in several major businesses, including those that produce machinery for the railroad and industry, hand and machine tools, chemicals, tires, vehicles, and paper. As a result of this adaptation, the city is still quite vibrant and significant to the Spanish economy.

6. There are several beautiful structures in Bilbao's old district.

You already know that Bilbao is essentially split into two sections: industry and commerce.

The ancient and historic part of Bilbao is lovely and full of marvels. It is located on the western side, which is the right bank of the Nervión River (it flows from the North). The "Siete Calles," or "Seven Streets," which run parallel to one another and into the river, make up its central portion. The Plaza Nueva, the San Antonio, San Juanes, and San Nicholas churches, as well as the Cathedral of Santiago, are further notable locations.

7. Before the city's establishment in 1300, the region was inhabited.

After significant investigation, historians and archaeologists concluded that Bilbao's present location was inhabited before the city was founded in 1300.

There were several habitations. Others were on the right side of the estuary, where there formerly was a seaport primarily devoted to trading in general, and others were in what is now Bilbao's ancient Quarter. Others were situated in what is now the city's ancient town ("Bilbao la Vieja").

So there you have it, the seven intriguing general facts about the Spanish city of Bilbao.

The Guggenheim Museum is up next.

Bilbao's Guggenheim Museum Information

The Guggenheim Museum is very well-known and fascinating in its own right. Thousands of people visit Bilbao each year attracted by its contemporary architecture.

8. Frank Gehry's proposals were followed in the construction of the Guggenheim Museum.

Frank Gehry, a Canadian-born Los Angeles architect, created some of the most well-known and legendary buildings in the country. The New World Symphony in Miami is unquestionably one of them.

In 1991, Thomas Krens, the director of the Solomon R. Guggenheim Foundation, chose

Frank Gehry and his company, which is now known as Gehry Partners, to design the museum. There were several bids from throughout the globe, but Gehry was ultimately selected.

9. A monarch gave the Guggenheim Museum it's official opening.

The "most important piece of architecture" according to the 52 expert studies for Vanity Fair was this marvelously odd and gorgeous skyscraper. The fact that the Spanish king inaugurated it makes it much more spectacular!

From 1975 until 2014, Juan Carlos reigned as King of Spain. On October 17, 1997, he formally opened the renowned museum.

10. There are two other Guggenheim Museums that are open year-round.

You may not be aware of this, but the Solomon R. Guggenheim includes Bilbao's Guggenheim Museum. This benefactor established the organization in 1937 and has a sizable art collection.

In 1959, 10 years after Guggenheim's passing, New York City saw the opening of its first permanent museum. In 1951, a different one known as "The Peggy Guggenheim Collection" debuted in Venice, Italy.

CONVINCING REASONS FOR TOURISTS TO VISIT BILBAO

The dynamic city of Bilbao, located in the center of the Basque Country, provides a mesmerizing fusion of ancient history, cutting-edge design, and a flourishing cultural environment. Bilbao has become a popular vacation destination for tourists from all over the globe due to its distinctive appeal and plenty of attractions. We shall examine some of the most compelling reasons for tourists to go to Bilbao in this post.

1. Rich Cultural Heritage: Bilbao is a city with a strong connection to its past. It proudly honors its Basque culture, language, and traditions. By touring the ancient Casco Viejo (Old Town), with its winding alleyways, quaint squares, and traditional Basque architecture, visitors can fully

immerse themselves in the lively Basque culture. The city's various festivals, such as Aste Nagusia, an annual nine-day celebration packed with music, dance, and Basque sports, show how strongly the Basque people identify with and value their cultural history.

2. Architectural Wonders: Bilbao has an amazing fusion of architectural styles, from ancient monuments to cutting-edge modern buildings. Santiago Calatrava created the magnificent white footbridge known as the Zubizuri Bridge to link the city's two banks over the Nervión River.

Another remarkable piece of architecture is the Euskalduna Palace, a former shipyard turned conference and entertainment venue. In addition, the Basilica of Begona, which is built on a hill above the city, provides a breathtaking Gothic architecture in addition to panoramic views. A compelling urban scene is created in Bilbao by the contrast between the city's ancient and contemporary buildings.

3. Bilbao is a culinary haven, and Basque cuisine is famous for its high quality and distinctive tastes. There are several pintxos bars in the city where you may savor small-batch culinary masterpieces while sipping local wine or cider. Pintxos come in many varieties, from succulent fish that has just been cooked to savory Basque cheeses and tantalizing charcuterie.

Additionally, Bilbao is home to several Michelin-starred eateries that highlight the creative and sophisticated side of Basque cuisine. A genuine immersion into Basque culture and a treat for the taste senses is to explore the city's culinary scene.

4. Outdoor Recreation: Bilbao's position between the sea and the mountains provides tourists with a wide variety of outdoor recreational opportunities as well as breathtaking natural scenery. There are many hiking options in the neighboring mountains, with routes leading to stunning vistas and verdant valleys. A picturesque journey on the Artxanda Funicular takes you to the summit of Mount Artxanda,

where you can take in expansive views of the city and its surroundings. The lovely beaches of Sopelana and Plentzia, where you may unwind, swim, or engage in water sports, are close by for those wanting a seaside experience.

5. The Nervión River weaves its way through Bilbao, enhancing the city's attractiveness and providing a distinctive ambiance. Beautiful architectural structures like the Guggenheim Museum and the Zubizuri Bridge line the riverbanks, making for a magnificent backdrop for strolls or bike rides along the riverside.

Visitors may discover the city's riverbank splendor while taking in the peace and greenery along the Bilbao Riverwalk, a pedestrian walkway that runs beside the river. The river also provides a background for a variety of cultural activities and festivals, enhancing the city's vivacious spirit.

6. A flourishing arts and entertainment scene that appeals to all interests can be found in Bilbao. You may catch live music, dance

performances, and theatrical shows at the city's many theaters, concert halls, and performance spaces.

Additionally, Bilbao holds several music events throughout the year, including anything from rock and electronic music to jazz and classical music. There are several galleries and exhibition halls that feature both domestic and foreign artists for art lovers. The street art and sculptures that dot the metropolitan environment provide a touch of inventiveness to every corner, enhancing the city's creative energy.

7. Bilbao has a variety of local boutiques, designer shops, and cutting-edge fashion districts, making it a shoppers' paradise. The annual Bilbao Fashion Week, when both up-and-coming and established designers exhibit their most recent works, is held in the city, which is renowned for its fashion-forward aesthetic.

The Gran Va is a popular shopping district dotted with a variety of stores offering anything from high-end clothing to one-of-a-kind trinkets and regional crafts. You may learn about Bilbao's sense of style and bring fashionable souvenirs home by exploring the city's retail scene.

8. Day trips to the Basque Country: Bilbao is a great home base for seeing the region's varied natural beauties. You may go a short distance to the coastal towns of San Sebastian and Getxo, which are renowned for their beautiful beaches, lively promenades, and delectable gastronomic scenes. Bermeo and Lekeitio, two little fishing communities, provide a window into typical Basque sea life.

Additionally, wine lovers wishing to engage in vineyard tours and tastings may easily go to the Rioja wine area, known for its top-notch wines. The advantageous position of Bilbao makes it possible to take amazing day excursions that give visitors a taste of the area's natural and cultural assets.

To wrap it up, Bilbao is an alluring location that skillfully combines history, culture, food, and unspoiled beauty. Bilbao provides a distinctive and engaging experience for every tourist, from its recognizable monuments and architectural wonders to its thriving cultural scene and gastronomic pleasures.

The city is an appealing destination that should be on every traveler's itinerary because of its friendly people, breathtaking scenery, and rich cultural history. It doesn't matter whether you're looking for outdoor activities, art, and culture, or just a taste of Basque friendliness, Bilbao guarantees a fantastic trip full of fascinating discoveries and indelible memories.

CHAPTER 2

STRUCTURING A PROFITABLE TRAVEL TO BILBAO

Travelers will find a multitude of sights, cultural opportunities, and gastronomic pleasures in Bilbao, the energetic city at the center of the Basque Country. Planning beforehand is crucial for a successful and pleasant vacation to Bilbao.

Here are some of the things to take into account when planning:

1. Choose the Best Time to Visit: The time of your visit to Bilbao may have a big influence on how you feel about it. The city has a pleasant temperature all year long, however, the summer (June to September) season is often the busiest with more visitors and more expensive lodging. Consider going in the spring (April to May) or fall (September to October) if you want fewer tourists and nicer weather.

Remember that Bilbao organizes several festivals and cultural events all year long; thus, it is worthwhile to check the calendar of events to see if any festivities interest you.

2. Research the Must-See Attractions and Activities in Bilbao to Create an Itinerary That Suits Your Interests. Plan Your Trip Ahead of Time. Among the attractions worth mentioning are the renowned Guggenheim Museum, the illustrious Casco Viejo (Old Town), and the breathtaking Zubizuri Bridge. Give yourself enough time to take in the city's museums, art galleries, and cultural history.

3. Safe Accommodation: Bilbao provides a variety of lodging choices to fit every need and taste. The city center is a well-liked option since it offers quick access to the main attractions and a lively ambiance. However, if you want a more tranquil setting, you may think about staying in the adjacent neighborhoods or even in nearby seaside towns, which provide a more laid-back atmosphere. To guarantee the greatest offers and

availability, do your research and make your hotel reservations well in advance.

4. Navigating the city and its surroundings is simple because of Bilbao's effective public transit system, which includes buses, trams, and a metro network. Purchase a rechargeable transit card that can be used on several means of transportation, like the Barik card. If you want flexibility and access to more isolated regions if you want to travel the area extensively, renting a vehicle may help. But be aware that parking in the city's core may be scarce and pricey.

5. Although many Bilbao residents understand English, it's always beneficial to learn a few fundamental Spanish or Basque words to improve your contacts with the locals. Respecting the language and culture of the Basque people, who take great pride in their history, will help you have a more enjoyable journey. Learn the conventions and etiquette of welcoming someone with a handshake or a kiss on both cheeks.

6. Currency and Money Issues: The Euro (EUR) is the official currency of Bilbao and all of Spain. Make sure you have adequate local money on hand for modest purchases in areas that may not take credit cards, such as public transit or street sellers. You may easily withdraw money when required thanks to the city's many ATMs. To prevent any problems with your cards, let your bank know about your trip intentions.

7. Try the Local Cuisine: Bilbao provides a broad variety of eating alternatives to tempt your taste buds. Basque cuisine is known for its quality and tastes across the globe. Try pintxos, which are little nibbles often served on skewers or pieces of bread and are the Basque equivalent of tapas. Indulge in a gastronomic experience while jumping from one pintxo bar to another in the Casco Viejo area, savoring a selection of delectable pintxos paired with regional wines or cider. Don't pass up the chance to sample authentic Basque cuisines such as ganguro (spider crab) and bacalao al pil-pil (codfish in olive oil and garlic sauce). It's also important to

look around the neighborhood markets, like the Mercado de la Ribera, where you can discover a wide selection of fish, cheeses, and fresh veggies to make your culinary creations.

8. For ease and safety, it's essential to maintain connectivity when traveling in Bilbao. Consult your cell service provider about your alternatives for international roaming, or think about getting a local SIM card for talking and Internet use. In Bilbao, the majority of hotels, cafés, and restaurants have free Wi-Fi, enabling you to keep in touch and tell others about your experiences. Use navigation applications or download offline maps to help you navigate the city without constant internet connectivity.

9. Study Local Customs and Etiquette: Get to know the customs and etiquette of the area before visiting Bilbao to ensure a pleasant and respectful encounter. Being on time for meetings and reservations is crucial since the Basque people value courtesy and timeliness. It is traditional to say "Hola" or "Kaixo" to the bartender or waiter upon entering a pintxos bar,

as well as "por favor" (please) and "gracias" (thank you) while dealing with locals. Common politeness habits include respecting others' personal space and minimizing loudness in public areas.

10. While careful preparation is essential for a good vacation, it's also critical to make space for flexibility and to accept serendipity. Allow yourself to ramble around Bilbao's lovely alleyways, discover undiscovered treasures, and partake in unplanned encounters. Talk to the people, get their advice, and be willing to try new things. So embrace the experience and let Bilbao surprise you—some of the most memorable moments throughout your vacation may come from unexpected interactions or discoveries.

11. Consider the weather and your intended activities while selecting your clothing for your vacation to Bilbao. It's a good idea to pack layers that you can simply add or remove since the weather may change quickly. For touring the city's sights and traversing its picturesque

cobblestone streets, you must wear comfortable walking shoes. For your excursions, remember to include a day bag filled with necessities like sunscreen, a refillable water bottle, and a map or guidebook.

Careful planning, thorough preparation, and a willingness to embrace Bilbao's distinctive culture and experiences are all necessary for a successful vacation there.

You can make your trip memorable and fulfilling by taking into account aspects like the ideal time to go, planning an agenda that includes a variety of activities, learning about local cultures, and keeping connected. Prepare yourself to experience Bilbao's intriguing atmosphere, breathtaking architecture, delectable food, and kind hospitality.

CHAPTER 3

BEST TIME FOR TRAVELERS TO VISIT BILBAO

The whole year may be enjoyed in Bilbao, the cultural center of the Basque Country in northern Spain. Every tourist may find something to enjoy in Bilbao thanks to its pleasant temperature, extensive history, and dynamic cultural scene. Nevertheless, depending on your tastes and interests, several seasons of the year are said to be the greatest for traveling.

Spring (April to June): Spring is a great season to go to Bilbao since the city wakes to blossom flowers and better weather. 15°C to 20°C (59°F to 68°F) is the typical daily temperature, which is comfortable for outdoor activities and seeing the city's attractions. In addition to being less congested, the springtime offers a chance to visit major locations like the Guggenheim Museum and Casco Viejo (Old Town) without the throng. Since spring in Bilbao falls during the pintxos season, when pubs and restaurants present their best culinary creations, it's also a terrific time for foodies.

Summer (July to September): Tourists from all over the world swarm to Bilbao throughout the summer to take advantage of the pleasant weather and vibrant environment. 20°C to 25°C (68°F to 77°F) is the typical temperature range, with brief increases to higher levels. Since there are more daylight hours throughout the summer, you have more time to explore and engage in outdoor activities.

It's crucial to remember that the summer months are also the busiest for visitor groups, particularly during the Aste Nagusia festival, a nine-day event that features music, dancing, and Basque sports. Summer might be a great season to visit Bilbao if you don't mind the crowds and prefer a lively environment.

Autumn (October to November): Autumn is the best season for people looking for a more laid-back and calmer experience in Bilbao since it provides lower weather and fewer visitors. At the start of the season, the average temperature is between 15°C and 20°C (59°F and 68°F), progressively decreasing as November draws near. Beautiful fall foliage characterizes Bilbao's autumn season, providing a magnificent background for your tour of the city. It's a wonderful time to stroll around parks like Dona Casilda Park and take in the vibrant landscape. Additionally, the adjacent Rioja wine region's harvest season occurs in the fall, giving wine lovers the chance to take part in vineyard excursions and tastings.

Winter (December to February): In comparison to other European cities, Bilbao's winters are relatively moderate, with daytime highs of 8°C to 14°C (46°F to 57°F). Winter in Bilbao has its special appeal, even if it may not be the warmest season to visit. The city is exquisitely decked up for the holidays, with merry lights illuminating the avenues and public spaces. You may enjoy the city's attractions in a more laid-back and private atmosphere during the winter thanks to reduced accommodation prices and fewer visitors. Winter is a great time to visit Bilbao's interior attractions, including its museums and art galleries, and to savor the city's delectable cuisine, which includes substantial Basque meals that will make you feel warm when it's cold.

Overall, your choices and interests will determine when is the ideal time to go to Bilbao. Summer may be the best season to come if you want warm temperatures, exciting events, and a buzzing environment.

Spring and fall both provide excellent weather and a more laid-back atmosphere for people who like acclimating to warmer temperatures and fewer crowds. For those looking for a more sedate and private vacation, winter offers a distinctive experience with discounted prices and a festive ambiance.

Bilbao is a year-round destination, and each has its unique benefits and attractions. This is crucial to keep in mind. Consider elements like your preferred weather, the number of visitors, and any events or activities that may be of interest to you when making your travel arrangements.

Additionally, bear in mind that Bilbao's position in the Basque Country provides the chance to go beyond the city's boundaries. Popular vacation spots with stunning beaches and lively communities include the adjacent coastal villages of San Sebastian and Getxo. For wine connoisseurs, the nearby Rioja wine region, with its vineyards and wineries, provides a great experience.

Take into account the following advice to get the most out of your trip to Bilbao:

1. Check the neighborhood events schedule; Bilbao has several festivals and cultural events all year long. Find out when these activities are taking place, then decide whether you want to participate. Your journey may become even more exciting and culturally immersive as a result.

2. Be prepared for long lines at famous sites: Especially during high season, several of

Bilbao's prominent attractions, like the Guggenheim Museum, may have lengthy lines. To avoid lines and guarantee a pleasant visit, think about ordering your tickets online ahead of time or getting there early.

3. Dress appropriately: Since the weather in Bilbao is erratic, it's best to bring clothes and be ready for a range of temperatures throughout the day. Even in the summer, bring a light jacket or sweater since it might become chilly at night.

4. As Bilbao is recognized for its extensive Basque past, it is important that you experience the local food and culture while you are there. To learn more about the rich culture of the city, try traditional Basque cuisine, visit the pintxos pubs in Casco Viejo, and interact with the people.

5. Be flexible with your itinerary: While having a broad plan for your trip is vital, you should also give yourself some leeway. The best parts of a vacation are often unexpected events and coincidental discoveries. Allow for impromptu

discoveries and don't be scared to stray from your predetermined course.

Bilbao is a fascinating city with year-round attractions for all types of visitors. Whether you like the summer's exuberant spirit, the autumn's beautiful landscape, the winter's merry vibe, or the spring's balmy temps, Bilbao will welcome you with its distinct charm and variety of activities. To guarantee a memorable and pleasurable visit to this magnificent Basque city, take into account your interests, investigate the various seasons, and organize your trip appropriately.

WHAT SHOULD A TOURIST BRING WITH THEM?

Traveling as a tourist requires careful planning and effective packing to ensure you have everything you need and that your baggage is manageable. Even though precise products may differ based on your location and personal tastes, the following are important things to pack:

1. Clothing:

• Comfy walking shoes: Select supportive, comfy footwear that is appropriate for exploring and covering long distances.

• Pack clothes that are suited for the weather at your location, such as breathable, lightweight alternatives for warm weather or layering garments for lower temps.

• Swimwear: Don't forget to carry your swimsuit if your location has beaches or swimming chances.

• Rain gear: Depending on the time of year and the location, think about packing an umbrella or lightweight waterproof jacket to keep you dry during sudden downpours.

2. Travel papers:

• Passport and ID: Make sure you have a current passport and any other required travel-related identity papers.

• Visas and travel authorizations: Bring any essential visas or authorizations, if your destination requires them, and have them close to hand.

• Itinerary and reservations for your trip: Print or store electronic copies of your itinerary, hotel bookings, and any pre-scheduled excursions.

• Health insurance and emergency contact information: Keep a copy of the emergency contact information for both your home country and your destination with you at all times, as well as your health insurance card.

3. Gadgets and electronics

• Mobile phone and charger: Keep your phone and charger close by so you can communicate and use travel-related applications.

• Cameras and memory cards: Use a camera or the camera on your smartphone to record your trip experiences. Keep extra memory cards and external storage in mind.

Bring the proper adapters and converters for your gadgets if you're visiting a place with multiple types of electrical outlets.

4. Personal Preferences:

• Toiletries: Bring travel-sized versions of your essential personal care products, including toothpaste, a toothbrush, shampoo, and conditioner.

• prescriptions: Bring any required prescription drugs, along with a compact first-aid kit filled with basic supplies like bandages, painkillers, and any other prescriptions you may need.

• Sunscreen and insect repellent: Pack sunscreen and insect repellent to protect your skin from sunburn and pesky insects.

• Travel-sized laundry detergent: Pack a modest quantity of travel-sized laundry detergent if you want to wash laundry while on vacation.

• Travel towel: If you want to visit beaches or partake in water sports, a lightweight, quick-drying travel towel may come in handy.

5. Capital and safety:

Carry a combination of cash and cards for easy and safe transactions. To prevent any problems using your card, let your bank know about your trip intentions.

• Money belt or concealed pouch: To protect your valuables and critical papers, think about wearing a covert money belt or concealed pouch.

• Travel locks: Pack compact travel locks to protect your belongings in hotel or hostel lockers.

6. Amusement and comfort

• Maps or travel guides: Use maps or travel guides to find your way around and learn essential information.

Have some reading material with you for lengthy flights or downtime when traveling, such as books, periodicals, or an e-reader.

• Travel pillow and eye mask: Using a travel cushion and eye mask can help you feel more comfortable on long flights or train trips.

To make your vacations more pleasant and to allow space for souvenirs, keep in mind to pack lightly and avoid overpacking. Make your packing list fit the unique activities and cultural customs of your trip.

CHAPTER 4

BILBAO'S ACCOMMODATION AND TRANSPORTATION OPTIONS

The accommodation you choose to stay in should be one of your top priorities when making travel plans to Bilbao. Fortunately, the city provides a variety of alternatives to meet the requirements and tastes of every visitor. For travelers searching for a cozy and practical place to stay, Bilbao offers a wide range of accommodations, from five-star hotels to inexpensive hostels. Here are some accommodation options for tourists:

1. Luxury Hotels: Bilbao is home to several upscale hotels that cater to affluent visitors looking for a lavish and opulent experience. These hotels often provide classy guestrooms and suites with deluxe amenities, exemplary service, and on-site attractions like spas, fitness centers, and fine eating establishments. The Gran Hotel Domine Bilbao, Hotel Carlton, and Hotel Meliá Bilbao are a few of Bilbao's

well-known luxury hotels. For those who are ready to spend more, these businesses provide the ideal balance of convenience, elegance, and excellent service, guaranteeing a wonderful visit.

2. Boutique Hotels: Bilbao offers a variety of attractive boutique hotels for tourists who desire a more private and distinctive lodging experience. These more intimate establishments often have chic, uniquely designed rooms that showcase the city's thriving creative and cultural landscape.

Bilbao's boutique hotels are renowned for their meticulous attention to detail, individualized service, and inviting atmosphere. The Hotel Miró, Hotel Palacio de Oriol, and Hotel Conde Duque are a few well-known examples of boutique hotels. Visitors may fully experience Bilbao's unique character while also taking advantage of the comfort and exclusivity of a boutique hotel while staying there.

3. Mid-Range Hotels: For tourists looking for a compromise between comfort and budget,

mid-range hotels are a popular option. Several mid-range hotels in Bilbao provide cozy lodging, cutting-edge facilities, and affordable pricing. These lodgings are a great choice for visiting the city since they are often conveniently situated close to popular sites. Mid-range lodgings like Hotel Silken Indautxu, Hotel NH Collection Villa de Bilbao, and Hotel Ercilla provide cozy accommodations, excellent service, and a pleasurable stay without breaking the bank.

4. Budget-Friendly Hotels and Hostels: Bilbao offers a wide selection of hotels and hostels that are suitable for travelers on a limited budget. These lodgings provide reasonable choices without sacrificing convenience and comfort. Budget hotels in Bilbao provide straightforward facilities, spotless lodging, and a convenient location, making them the perfect choice for those who want to maximize city exploration while keeping costs down.

Hostels, on the other hand, provide a social and communal environment, sometimes with shared dormitory-style rooms, common spaces, and the chance to meet other visitors. Hotels and hostels in Bilbao that are affordable include the Hotel Bilbi, Pension Don Claudio, and Bilbao Akelarre Hostel.

5. Apartment rentals are a great option for anyone looking for a home-away-from-home atmosphere. For guests who want their own home with a kitchen and living room, Bilbao provides a variety of flats and holiday rentals. Families or bigger parties who like the freedom of preparing their meals and having more space to spread around might choose this option. Apartment rentals in Bilbao are available on websites like Airbnb and Booking.com, where visitors may choose from a range of options for size, location, and cost.

6. Staying in a casa rural, or rural home, might be the ideal choice if you're hoping to get away from the city and take in Bilbao's picturesque surroundings. These lodgings are often found in the lovely countryside, providing a peaceful getaway from the busy metropolis. Staying in a casa rural, or rural home, might be the ideal

choice if you're hoping to get away from the city and take in Bilbao's picturesque surroundings. These lodgings are often found in the lovely countryside, providing a peaceful getaway from the busy metropolis.

The Basque Country's rural charm may be experienced while still being close to Bilbao's attractions thanks to casas rurales. These historic homes often have charming restorations, rustic exteriors, and warm interiors. They include a variety of facilities including fully functional kitchens, private patios or gardens, and sometimes even swimming pools.

Visitors may take part in outdoor activities like cycling and trekking while staying in a rural area, or they can just relax and take in the area's natural beauty. Families, nature enthusiasts, and anybody else looking for a tranquil, immersive experience should consider it.

Camping & campsites: For outdoorsy, adventurous tourists, camping in Bilbao might be a fun choice. The area has several fully-equipped campgrounds that welcome RV and camper enthusiasts. These campgrounds provide amenities including roomy pitches, power hookups, spotless bathrooms, and sometimes even swimming pools and leisure areas.

Camping enables you to take advantage of the area's natural beauty, allowing you to wake up to breathtaking views and clean air. It's a fantastic option for anybody looking for a cheap and in-the-moment encounter. Camping Arrien, Camping Urrobi, and Camping Itxaspe are a few of the well-known campgrounds in Bilbao.

When selecting a hotel in Bilbao, it's crucial to take accessibility into account, particularly for those with special needs or mobility concerns. For visitors with impairments, the city's hotels and flats have accessible rooms or amenities. It is best to get in touch with the lodging directly to find out about accessible amenities and make sure they can accommodate your demands.

Consider where your selected lodging is about nearby attractions and public transit alternatives as well. Your overall experience and convenience of traveling about the city may be improved by selecting a place that is centrally located or close to easily accessible public transit.

Best Hotels in Bilbao

Finding the ideal hotel is crucial when making travel plans to Bilbao to guarantee a relaxing and pleasurable stay. The city has a variety of lodging choices, including high-end hotels, quaint boutique properties, and affordable alternatives. We have put together a list of the best 10 hotels in Bilbao, each providing its own special charm and first-rate service, to assist you in making an educated choice.

1. The magnificent and contemporary Gran Hotel Domine Bilbao is located directly across from the renowned Guggenheim Museum and is renowned for its excellent position and breathtaking views. Stylish guests love the

hotel's accommodation sizes, expansive layouts, and first-rate facilities, which include a rooftop terrace and a fine dining restaurant.

2. Hotel Carlton: The Hotel Carlton is a well-known landmark in Bilbao and has magnificent Belle Époque architecture. This five-star hotel offers roomy accommodations, a fitness facility, and a famous restaurant while fusing traditional design with contemporary conveniences. Its popularity is heightened by its strategic placement, adjacent to the city's top tourist destinations and commercial districts.

3. In the center of Bilbao's commercial sector, the Hotel Meliá Bilbao mixes modern architecture with welcoming service. It is a well-liked option for both business and leisure tourists because of its chic accommodations, first-rate service, and rooftop spa center with panoramic views.

4. Hotel Miró: The Hotel Miró exudes artistic refinement and is situated in Bilbao's cultural area. Original artwork is displayed throughout

the contemporary guest rooms and public areas of this boutique hotel. It stands out as a great option for art fans because of its strategic location, attentive service, and rooftop patio with stunning views.

5. Hotel Palacio de Oriol: This ancient jewel is set in a gorgeously renovated palace and is located in the seaside town of Santurce, not far from Bilbao. The hotel's exquisite rooms, which are furnished with antiques, provide a window into the lengthy history of the area. It offers a tranquil retreat from the city because of its beautiful surroundings and proximity to the beach.

6. The Hotel Ercilla is a well-known landmark in the heart of Bilbao and has a long-standing reputation for excellence and comfort. A pleasurable stay is guaranteed by its contemporary accommodations, excellent service, and variety of facilities, which include a rooftop pool and several eating choices. The hotel's charm is enhanced by its handy position close to the Old Town.

7. Hotel Silken Indautxu: Located in the Indautxu district, this hotel provides a modern and chic atmosphere. Travelers seeking a contemporary and pleasant stay often choose the hotel because of its sleek rooms, spa center, and restaurant featuring Basque cuisine.

8. In the heart of the city, the Hotel NH Collection Villa de Bilbao mixes a contemporary aesthetic with a warm environment. A comfortable stay is guaranteed by the hotel's room sizes, fitness facility, and an on-site restaurant offering regional delicacies. Another benefit is that the hotel is close to the Guggenheim Museum and other attractions.

9. Hotel Abando: Located in the center of Bilbao, the Hotel Abando is a good starting point for exploring the area. Its cozy accommodations, helpful staff, and chic lobby with a glass dome all contribute to the hotel's pleasant atmosphere. The hotel is well situated for sightseeing and shopping, being just a short stroll from the Old Town.

10. Near Bilbao's renowned theater, the Hotel Sercotel Coliseo combines contemporary comfort with classic charm. The hotel is popular among tourists looking for a comfortable and convenient place to stay because of its roomy accommodations, stylish design, and a rooftop terrace with views of the whole city.

All of these hotels profit from Bilbao's energetic environment and diverse cultural offers in addition to their distinctive attractions. Guests staying at these hotels enjoy quick access to the city's most famous buildings and attractions, whether they want to explore the famed Guggenheim Museum or just walk around the Old Town's lovely streets.

Many of these hotels have fantastic restaurants that provide a wide selection of delectable foods. Without leaving the comfort of their hotel, visitors may indulge in a culinary experience including everything from traditional Basque cuisine to worldwide delicacies. Some hotels even include rooftop dining choices, enabling guests to appreciate their meals while taking in the surrounding scenery.

The top 10 hotels in Bilbao also take great pleasure in their outstanding service and helpful employees. The hotel team is committed to making sure visitors have a pleasant and stress-free stay, whether you need help with buying tickets for a play or suggestions for close-by activities.

It's important to note that Bilbao draws tourists all year long, so it's a good idea to book reservations in advance, particularly during busy travel times or for certain events. By doing this, you may be sure to reserve your favorite hotel and the dates you want to visit this fascinating city.

The best 10 hotels in Bilbao provide a variety of alternatives to suit every taste and budget, whether you're a luxury visitor, an art fan, or a money-conscious traveler. You may make your trip to Bilbao even better and leave with enduring memories by selecting one of these first-rate lodging options.

Bilbao's Transportation Options

With its effective and practical transit alternatives, Bilbao is a delight to navigate when visiting. Bilbao has a variety of options that respond to various requirements and tastes, whether you prefer public transit or exploring on foot. Check the following transportation options:

1. Metro: The Bilbao Metro is a well-liked and dependable means of transportation that offers speedy and effective movement across the city and its environs. The metro network consists of two lines, Line 1 and Line 2, which link important landmarks, neighborhoods, and commercial sectors. The metro is a great option for touring Bilbao's biggest attractions, including the Guggenheim Museum, the Old Town, and the Casco Viejo area since it has regular trains and well-connected stops.

2. Euskotren Tranbia, Bilbao's tram system, provides a practical means to go about the city's

core and its suburbs. The tram network is a practical choice for both inhabitants and visitors since it serves well-known locations like Atxuri, Abando, and La Casilla. Modern trams are accessible and comfortable, making for a nice ride while taking in city vistas. The tram system also links to the bus and subway lines, enabling easy transitions between various types of transportation.

3. Bus: The vast bus network in Bilbao covers the whole city and its surroundings. The bus service, which is run by Bilbobus, has a wide range of routes and is a great way to go to places that aren't accessible by tram or metro. In Bilbao, buses are renowned for their regularity and timeliness, making it simple to travel to different neighborhoods, commercial areas, and tourist sites. Tourists may easily traverse the system since bus stations are well-signposted and route maps are provided.

4. Bilbao Bizkaia Card: The Bilbao Bizkaia Card is a fantastic choice for those who want to experience not just Bilbao but also the larger

Bizkaia area. This card grants unrestricted use of all public transportation in Bilbao and the rest of the province, including the metro, tram, and bus services. Additionally, it provides deals and free entrance to a variety of tourist destinations, museums, and guided tours. The Bilbao Bizkaia Card comes in a variety of lengths, letting travelers choose the one that best fits their schedule.

5. Walking: Since Bilbao is a pedestrian-friendly city, many of its attractions may be reached on foot from one. You may completely immerse yourself in the city's energetic ambiance and find hidden jewels while exploring it on foot. Bilbao's streets are kept up properly and have sidewalks that are suitable for strollers, so it is secure and fun to do so. The city's architecture, street art, and lovely districts can all be seen up close when you're out walking.

6. Bicycle: Bilbao has a bike-sharing program called Bilbao Bizi for individuals who would want a more active and environmentally responsible method to tour the city. Visitors may

hire bicycles for a limited time at one of the many docking stations spread out across the city and explore Bilbao at their speed. Additionally, the city has designated bicycle lanes that make it safe and simple for bicycles to go through traffic. By renting a bicycle, you may get a fresh perspective on Bilbao's attractions and go farther while taking in the great outdoors.

7. Taxis and ride-sharing services are widely accessible in Bilbao, and they provide a practical and pleasant means of transportation, particularly for people who are carrying baggage or want a more private and direct trip. Taxis may be located at authorized taxi ranks or hailed from the street anywhere in the city.

Taxi drivers in Bilbao are often amiable and informed about the city, and the vehicles are fitted with meters to ensure clear pricing. Popular choices like Uber and Cabify are also accessible in Bilbao if you prefer the comfort of ride-sharing services as an alternative to conventional taxis.

8. Renting a vehicle: In Bilbao, renting a vehicle provides you the flexibility to go about and take in the beautiful scenery of the Basque Country as well as the city itself. In Bilbao, several car rental agencies provide a variety of automobiles to fit various demands and price ranges.

With a vehicle, you may go outside of the city to attractive coastal villages, gorgeous beaches, and breathtaking countryside. Parking in the city center might be difficult, and certain locations can have rules or charges for parking, so it's vital to keep that in mind.

9. Consider taking a trip on a funicular or cable car for an unforgettable transportation experience and stunning views of Bilbao. Near the city's heart, the Artxanda Funicular transports visitors to Mount Artxanda, where they may enjoy sweeping views of Bilbao's cityscape.

Both residents and visitors enjoy riding the funicular, which is open throughout the day. The cable car that runs between Bilbao and the nearby town of Getxo is an additional alternative. This picturesque trip between the two destinations offers breathtaking views of the coastline and is an unforgettable experience.

10. Ferries and river cruises: From the Nervion River, Bilbao's position on the river provides a unique chance to see the city. Visitors may enjoy a relaxing boat ride while taking in the views thanks to the many ferry services and river cruises that run along the river.

These water-based modes of transportation provide a unique approach to take in Bilbao's architectural landmarks, such as the famous Guggenheim Museum and the charming riverside bridges.

Bilbao has a variety of transportation choices to suit various tastes and requirements. It is easy to get about the city thanks to the effective tram and subway systems, buses, taxis, and even bicycles.

It doesn't matter whether you decide to explore on foot, hire a vehicle for more freedom, or enjoy a gorgeous journey on the funicular or cable car—Bilbao's transit system makes it simple to get about and see the city's numerous sights and undiscovered gems.

CHAPTER 5

MAJOR ACTIVITIES FOR TOURISTS IN BILBAO

GOING TO A BEACH

The Guggenheim Museum, the bustling city streets, and Bilbao's rich cultural legacy are often the first things that spring to mind when one thinks of the city. However, Bilbao also has stunning beaches that are well worth seeing while you're there.

These beaches, which are tucked away along the scenic Bay of Biscay coastline, provide a welcome respite from the busy metropolis and an opportunity to relax in breathtaking natural settings. The best beaches in Bilbao, each with its distinct charm and attractiveness, are described in this article.

1. Playa de Ereaga is a well-liked vacation spot for both residents and tourists. It is situated in the coastal town of Getxo not far from Bilbao. There is enough access to beach activities like

picnics and sunbathing on this long, sandy beach, which is over a kilometer long. The beach is well-equipped with facilities, such as showers, restrooms, and lifeguard services, guaranteeing beachgoers a secure and pleasurable experience. Its allure is increased by the fact that tourists may explore the lively ambiance of the town after a day of sun and surf thanks to its closeness to the picturesque Old Port of Algorta and the energetic promenade of Ereaga.

2. Playa de Plentzia: This lovely beach, with its golden sands and clean waves, is located in the village of Plentzia, about 25 kilometers from Bilbao. It is a kid-friendly beach great for swimming, sandcastle-building, and sunbathing. This beach is a well-liked location for relaxation and leisurely walks along the seashore because of the serene ambiance and picturesque surroundings. The beach is a great choice for a day excursion to soak up the sun and take in the coastal atmosphere since it is quickly reachable from Bilbao by public transit.

3. Playa de Gorliz: Playa de Gorliz, a gorgeous beach recognized for its unspoiled natural beauty and serene atmosphere, is situated in the coastal community of Gorliz, about 30 kilometers from Bilbao. This sandy beach provides a tranquil hideaway where tourists may soak up the sun and take in the calming sound of the waves. It is surrounded by cliffs and lush hills.

The beach is kept up nicely and has facilities including restrooms, showers, and lifeguard coverage. In addition, the adjacent village of Gorliz has quaint cafés and eateries where you may enjoy delectable seafood meals while admiring the bay's expansive vistas.

4. Playa de Azkorri is a stunning, undeveloped beach that spans about 800 meters and is found near the municipality of Getxo. This beach provides a peaceful and natural environment that is ideal for nature enthusiasts since it is surrounded by rocky cliffs and thick flora.

Even though swimming is permitted, it's vital to remember that the sea currents may be powerful.

The beach is private and gorgeous, and it is accessible through a wooden stairway. For a fully immersive experience, visitors may also explore the adjacent rocky coves and go on coastal treks.

5. Playa de Arrigunaga is a picturesque urban beach well known for its beauty and recreational opportunities. It is located in the Algorta area of Getxo. This sandy beach has great amenities including showers, restrooms, and a kids' play area. It is ideal for sunbathing.

The renowned Arrigunaga Beach Balcony, a picturesque vantage point with expansive views of the coastline and the Bay of Biscay, is one of this beach's attractions. The beach is popular with surfers of all skill levels who wish to catch some waves because of the favorable surfing conditions.

6. Playa de Sopelana is a well-known beach among surfers and beach lovers and is located in the municipality of Sopelana, about 18 kilometers from Bilbao. This expansive section

of golden sand is a favorite location for surfing contests and events because of its reliable waves. The beach provides a wonderful setting for sunbathing, beach activities, and long walks down the coast since it is surrounded by towering cliffs and is backed by lush green hills. Playa de Sopelana has amenities including showers, restrooms, and lifeguard coverage to make sure that tourists have a safe and pleasurable time.

7. Playa de Barinatxe, sometimes referred to as La Salvaje is an undeveloped, untamed beach halfway between Sopelana and Getxo. Nature enthusiasts and those looking for a more untamed beach experience enjoy this remote sanctuary. Playa de Barinatxe has a special atmosphere that is ideal for nature hikes, photography, and reflection thanks to its rocky shoreline, dunes, and spectacular vistas. The beach is undeveloped, thus guests are recommended to bring their food, drink, and beach basics since there are no amenities on the beach.

8. A secret treasure that draws both residents and daring tourists is Playa de Arrieta-Atxabiribil, which is located in the village of Sopelana. This spotless beach is renowned for its stunning beauty and laid-back vibe. It provides the perfect backdrop for swimming, sunbathing, and beach activities because of its expansive sandy beachfront and clean seas.

The cliffs of Playa de Arrieta-Atxabiribil are good launch sites for paragliders, who use them to fly above the shoreline and take in the beautiful vistas. With close parking and amenities like restrooms, picnic spaces, and showers, the beach is conveniently located.

9. Playa de Bakio: This gorgeous beach, which is about 35 kilometers from Bilbao, has a mixture of sandy stretches and cliffs. This beach provides space for relaxing and water sports due to its length of shoreline. Playa de Bakio is especially well-liked by tourists due to its regular waves that are appropriate for surfers of all skill levels. Showers, restrooms, and beach bars are available at the beach, where guests may

relax with a drink while admiring the breathtaking coastline scenery. Bakio is a quaint seaside village that provides a variety of services, dining alternatives, and lodging choices.

10. Playa de Laga is a clean, undeveloped beach that displays the natural beauty of the Basque Country. It is located in the Urdaibai Biosphere Reserve. This sandy beach provides a serene and picturesque getaway from the busy city since it is surrounded by green cliffs and undulating hills.

Due to its proximity to wetlands and marshes where there are chances for birding, Playa de Laga is well-liked by outdoor lovers. Excellent swimming conditions are available at the beach itself, along with amenities including restrooms, showers, and lifeguard coverage. It's noteworthy that Playa de Laga has received the Blue Flag certification for excellence in environmental management and cleanliness.

As a result, Bilbao and the surrounding regions provide a wide variety of beaches that may be tailored to suit different tastes, from crowded metropolitan beaches to isolated and untamed stretches of sand. The best beaches in Bilbao provide the ideal location for a day of leisure in the sun, exhilarating water sports, or connecting with nature. So embrace and pack your beach necessities.

WHY PARTICIPATION ACTIVITIES ON THE BEACH

There are many activities and things to do at the beach that may improve your experience and help you make the most of your time by the water. Here are a few well-liked choices:

1. Relaxation and sunbathing are two of the most basic but pleasurable beach pastimes. Soak up the warmth of the sun. Apply sunscreen, set up a cozy chair or beach blanket, and then relax while taking in the tranquil sounds of the waves and the soft sea breeze. It's the ideal time to unwind

by reading a book, listening to music, meditating, or just napping.

2. Swimming & Water Sports: Enjoy the rush of swimming in open water while taking a cooling dip in the ocean. Water activities including surfing, bodyboarding, paddleboarding, kayaking, and snorkeling are best practiced along the beach.

To make the most of your beach vacation, rent equipment or sign up for a guided activity. Always make sure you are familiar with any local regulations or safety measures about water sports.

3. Play beach games with your family and friends to engage in some friendly rivalry. Beach volleyball, beach soccer, frisbee, badminton, or even a game of catch are all popular possibilities. In addition to being physically beneficial, these pursuits also foster laughter and enduring memories.

4. Building intricate sandcastles or sculptures out of the soft sand can let you express your

creativity. Use shovels, buckets, and other molds to give your idea life. It's a wonderful way to connect with kids or to indulge your inner child. Before the water takes away your inventions, remember to snap photographs of them.

5. Walk down the beach and explore it at your leisure while listening to the waves lapping at your feet. You may take in the natural beauty of the surroundings while walking on the beach, look for seashells, and experience the sand between your toes. Explore any tidal pools or rock formations that the beach may have to learn more about the wonderful marine life that lives there.

6. Beach barbecues & picnics: Prepare a mouthwatering spread for a beachfront BBQ or pack a tasty picnic. Bring your favorite sandwiches, snacks, fruits, and cool drinks with you. You may roll out a blanket on the sand or set out a picnic table and seat in a specified space at many beaches. Just be cautious of any rules governing burning or the disposal of rubbish.

7. Beach Yoga and Fitness: Work out or practice yoga on the sand to revitalize your body and mind. Yoga, meditation, and tai chi may all be practiced in a peaceful and inspirational environment on the beach. The soft sand may also make your workouts more difficult since it works various muscles and improves balance.

8. If there are restaurants, beach bars, or kiosks close to the beach, treat yourself to some delectable regional food or a cool beverage. Enjoy tropical drinks, ice cream, and delicious seafood while taking in the breathtaking vistas and beach vibe. Even better, you may enjoy your lunch without moving from your place thanks to certain beaches' beachfront service.

9. Observe the spectacular splendor of a beach sunset by sticking around until dusk. Find a cozy position on the sand or a beachside patio, and observe as the sky changes into a vibrantly colored artwork. It's a lovely moment that perfectly captures the peace and beauty of the beach in its natural state.

10. Environmental Preservation: As a considerate beachgoer, think about taking part in beach cleaning events or adopting eco-friendly practices. Use reusable water bottles and food containers, pick up any garbage you come across, and properly dispose of it.

Also, keep an eye out for animals and sensitive habitats. You can help keep the beach's natural beauty intact for future generations to enjoy if you respect the environment.

Many coastal towns sponsor beach cleaning events when volunteers join together to gather trash and other waste that might endanger marine life and degrade the beauty of the beach. Participating in these activities not only promotes environmental protection and contributes to keeping the beach clean.

11. Beach photography: Use your camera to record the breathtaking surroundings and memorable moments at the beach. The beach offers many opportunities for gorgeous photographs, whether you are using a

professional camera or a smartphone. Photography enables you to save memories and share them with others, from capturing the crashing waves and brilliant sunsets to candid images of friends and family having fun.

12. Beach bonfires: If allowed and in approved regions, taking part in a beach bonfire may be a special occasion. Spend time with loved ones while roasting marshmallows over a roaring fire and exchanging funny tales. An inviting and private ambiance is created by the fire's warmth and the sound of the waves.

13. Beaches are often home to a variety of marine and avian life. Seize the chance to check out the local fauna in its natural setting. If you're fortunate, you could see dolphins, sandpipers, crabs, and seagulls. To avoid interfering with their normal behavior, respect their space and keep your distance when observing.

14. Beach Festivals and Events: Look up any beach festivals or events scheduled to take place while you are there on the local events calendar.

These activities, which range from music festivals and beach gatherings to sporting events and cultural festivals, up the thrill level of your trip to the beach. Enjoy live performances, get to know the people, and socialize with tourists and residents alike.

15. Take use of the beach as a haven to practice mindfulness and relaxation exercises. Let go of any tension or anxieties as you take in the sounds of the ocean and the pleasant touch of the beach. Practice deep breathing, meditate, or just sit quietly and take in the peace of the beach setting.

Keep in mind that when participating in these activities, it's important to put safety first and observe all applicable beach laws and regulations. Pay attention to any warnings posted about the state of the water, the tides, or any prohibited places. To have a relaxing and pleasurable trip at the beach, be sure to carry your beach basics like sunscreen, hats, towels, and plenty of drinking water.

HISTORICAL SITES AND MONUMENTS YOU HAVE TO SEE

Bilbao, a thriving city in Spain's Basque Country, is well-known for both its contemporary architectural and cultural attractions as well as its extensive historical past.

There are many intriguing historical structures and monuments in Bilbao that provide insights into the city's history and historical development. Here are some of the noteworthy historical sites and monuments in Bilbao, ranging from prehistoric features to medieval buildings.

1. Santiago Cathedral, often known as Bilbao Cathedral, is a prominent religious and architectural monument that is situated in the center of the Old Town. The cathedral, which dates to the fourteenth century, combines Gothic, Renaissance, and Baroque architectural elements. It is a must-see for history and architectural fans because of its elaborate stone exterior, gorgeous stained glass windows, and

imposing altar. The grave of Don Diego López de Haro, the city's founder, is located within the cathedral along with several chapels and religious relics.

2. Plaza Nueva: Bilbao's Old Town's Plaza Nueva is a historic plaza that serves as a reminder of the city's history. This 19th-century neoclassical plaza has attractive buildings housing stores, pubs, and restaurants, as well as magnificent arcades, decorative balconies, and other architectural details. Since ancient times, Plaza Nueva has served as a focal point for key gatherings, festivals, and marketplaces. Visitors to this famous area may take in the bustling ambiance, savor the regional food, and marvel at the stunning architecture.

3. The huge theater known as Teatro Arriaga is situated in the heart of the city and is named after the well-known Basque musician Juan Crisóstomo Arriaga. The theater, which was constructed in the late 19th century and has an ornate interior and neo-baroque exterior, is an important cultural and historical relic. Since

more than a century ago, Teatro Arriaga has played home to various theatrical productions, operas, concerts, and ballets, drawing top performers and thrilling audiences. Visitors may view the opulent rooms, stage, and backstage parts of the theater on guided tours, which are offered.

4. Mercado de la Ribera: In addition to being Bilbao's biggest covered market, the Mercado de la Ribera is a historical treasure. It is a famous example of early 20th-century architecture and is situated on the banks of the Nervión River. The market's iron and glass building, which has an Art Nouveau feel to it, is home to a colorful assortment of vendors offering local specialties, handmade goods, and fresh fruit. Visitors may get a taste of the city's gastronomic heritage and enjoy the lively ambiance of a typical Spanish market by exploring the market.

5. The Basque Museum (Museo Vasco), which is situated in the Old Town, offers a thorough overview of the history, culture, and customs of the area. The museum is housed in a former

convent from the 17th century and has antiques, works of art, and records that illustrate the history of the Basque people. Visitors may discover more about Basque traditions, language, crafts, and the area's connection to the sea. The museum also arranges cultural activities, classes, and transient displays to better acquaint visitors with Basque culture.

6. La Ribera Market: The Mercado de la Ribera, usually referred to as La Ribera Market is a historically significant market that was established in the fourteenth century. It is one of the oldest covered marketplaces in Europe and is located on the outskirts of Casco Viejo (Old Town). With its iron framework and vibrant tiles, the market building is an architectural masterpiece in and of itself. Inside, there is a lively environment and a variety of vendors offering local goods including fresh fruit, meat, and seafood. The brilliant colors, alluring fragrances, and the sounds of merchants yelling out their products make La Ribera Market a sensory treat. In addition to giving you the

option to buy fresh goods, exploring the market gives you a chance to get to know the friendly merchants and get immersed in the community.

7. The Guggenheim Museum Bilbao is a historical monument on its own, although being largely recognized for its modern design. The museum's cutting-edge architecture, created by famous architect Frank Gehry and unveiled in 1997, has become a recognized representation of Bilbao's metamorphosis.

The museum is a showpiece of contemporary architecture with its titanium-clad facade and curved design. Inside, guests may peruse a sizable collection of modern artwork, which includes pieces by well-known creators like Jeff Koons, Andy Warhol, and Eduardo Chillida.

The architectural importance of the Guggenheim Museum Bilbao and its influence on the cultural environment of the city make it a must-see historical location.

8. The Vizcaya Bridge (Puente de Vizcaya), which is not far from Bilbao, is a UNESCO

World Heritage monument and a feat of engineering. It was the first transporter bridge ever constructed and was instrumental in uniting the two sides of the Nervión River when it was constructed in the late 19th century.

The bridge's distinctive design combines a gondola that resembles a ferry hanging on a metal framework to let both automobiles and people cross the river. On a gondola trip, visitors may take in expansive views of Bilbao and its surroundings. The Vizcaya Bridge is a reflection of Bilbao's industrial past and a monument to human inventiveness.

9. San Antón Church and Bridge: The San Antón Bridge, which crosses the Bilbao Estuary, is a famous historical building. One of Bilbao's oldest bridges, dates to the 13th century. The bridge provides beautiful views of the river and the region. The San Antón Church, a 15th-century structure in the Romanesque style, is located next to the bridge. Those who are interested in Bilbao's cultural legacy should

make a point of visiting the church because of its historic architecture and religious importance.

10. City Hall (Ayuntamiento): Located in the heart of Bilbao, the City Hall is a magnificent example of neo-baroque design. The early 20th-century structure has elaborate embellishments, imposing facades, and opulent interiors.

The City Hall, which houses the city's administration, is a significant representation of local pride. The building's architectural splendor may be seen from the exterior, or visitors can go inside to enjoy the common rooms and exhibits.

By highlighting the city's architectural, cultural, and industrial legacy, these historical locations and monuments in Bilbao provide visitors with a look into the past of the city. Visitors may understand Bilbao's transformation from a historic port city to a contemporary cultural center by seeing these sites. The historical attractions of Bilbao provide an enriching trip through time, whether it's admiring centuries-old churches, taking in the allure of traditional marketplaces, or being astounded by cutting-edge architectural wonders.

Most Important Outdoor Activities

In addition to its cultural landmarks and architectural marvels, Bilbao, located in the breathtaking Basque Country of Spain, provides a wide range of outdoor activities for adventurers and environment lovers. Here are some of the best outdoor activities to do in Bilbao, ranging from exploring natural landscapes to participating in exhilarating sports.

1. Hiking in the Basque Mountains: The gorgeous Basque Mountains around Bilbao, offer a wealth of attractions for hikers. Several routes in the close-by Gorbea Natural Park are suitable for hikers of all abilities. The climb up Mount Gorbea, the highest mountain in the Basque Country, is one well-liked route. Adventurers who complete the walk are rewarded with stunning panoramas of the nearby mountains and valleys. The Urkiola Natural Park

and the Armaón Natural Park, which both provide gorgeous paths through lush woods and stunning vistas, are two more well-known hiking locations.

2. Cycling along the Bilbao Riverwalk: Bilbao has a bustling riverbank district and a designated cycling route, making it the perfect place for a leisurely bike ride. Bicyclists can discover the city's stunning splendor while savoring the cool wind along the Nervión River's banks thanks to the Bilbao Riverwalk.

Rent a bike and ride along the trail, past famous sites like the Zubizuri Bridge, the Old Town, and the Guggenheim Museum Bilbao. Everyone of any age may enjoy riding because of the flat terrain and well-maintained infrastructure.

3. Mundaka is a seaside town known for its world-class surfing conditions, and it is just a short distance from Bilbao. The legendary "La Izquierda" left-hand wave, which draws surfers from all over the world in search of the ultimate thrill and adventure, is one of the most popular

waves in Mundaka. Even if you're not an experienced surfer, you can still take surf lessons at the nearby surf schools or enjoy watching the experts ride the waves. The breathtaking coastline and thriving surf scene in Mundaka make for an amazing outdoor adventure.

4. Kayaking on the Nervión River: Rent a kayak and paddle along the Nervión River to get a different view of Bilbao's cityscape. By floating by famous sites and taking in the peace of the sea, kayaking gives you a new perspective on the city. To cruise the river and see undiscovered areas of Bilbao, you may rent a kayak or sign up for a trip.

All ability levels may participate in this activity, which offers a wonderful chance to interact with nature while observing the city's beauty.

5. Paragliding in Artxanda provides breathtaking aerial views of Bilbao and its surroundings for thrill-seekers looking for a thrilling experience. From the charming Artxanda Hill, strap yourself into a paraglider and fly into the air while taking

in a bird's-eye view of the city and the surroundings. It's an outdoor sport you won't forget thanks to the knowledgeable paragliding instructors who guarantee your safety and lead you through the exhilarating trip.

6. Atxarte's limestone cliffs, which are close to Bilbao, are a great place for rock climbers to practice their craft. For climbers of all experience levels—beginners to experts—the region provides a range of routes. Atxarte provides a difficult and rewarding rock climbing experience because of its craggy cliffs and breathtaking natural surroundings.

Atxarte's rock faces provide an exhilarating outdoor sport, whether you're an experienced climber or a novice eager to take on a new challenge.

7. Sailing in the Bay of Biscay: Sail the waters of the Bay of Biscay to embrace Bilbao's nautical culture. Explore the coastline and revel in the fun of sailing by renting a boat or signing up for a sailing tour. With its clean seas, calm

winds, and lovely coastline scenery, the Bay of Biscay provides a lovely backdrop.

Sailing on the bay gives you the chance to take in the city's breathtaking shoreline and the tranquility of the open sea, whether you're an experienced sailor or a first-time explorer. On the deck, you may relax, enjoy the expansive views, and even try out boat steering with the assistance of seasoned sailors.

8. Enjoy a quiet picnic at Park Dona Casilda to get away from the hustle and bustle of the city. This vast green oasis, which is located in the center of Bilbao, provides a peaceful haven for those who like the outdoors.

Take a stroll around the park's well-kept gardens, pick a shady area, and have a picnic with your loved ones. The park's lovely flowerbeds, restful ponds, and statues provide a peaceful atmosphere for leisure. It's the ideal spot to relax, indulge in some delectable local food, and take in Bilbao's scenic surroundings.

9. Canyoning in the Oka Valley is a thrilling outdoor activity to think about if you're looking for an adrenaline-pumping experience. The Oka Valley, which is not far from Bilbao and features rocky terrain, steep gorges, and flowing waterfalls, is an excellent canyoning location. Swim through the valleys, leap into natural pools, and traverse riverbeds by rappelling down waterfalls. Leading the route are seasoned experts who guarantee your safety and give you an exhilarating adrenaline rush.

10. Birdwatching at the Urdaibai Biosphere Reserve: The Urdaibai Biosphere Reserve, close to Bilbao, will enchant nature lovers and bird watchers. This protected area is a birdwatcher's heaven since it is home to a wide variety of bird species. A variety of avian species, including herons, ospreys, spoonbills, and numerous migratory birds, may be seen in the marshes, estuaries, and woodlands if you grab your binoculars and go exploring. You may see these amazing animals in their natural environment

thanks to the reserve's well-marked pathways and viewing platforms.

Everyone may find something to enjoy in Bilbao's outdoor activities, from exhilarating experiences to tranquil nature getaways. The outdoor attractions in Bilbao provide the ideal blend of excitement, relaxation, and exposure to the city's natural beauty, whether you like climbing in the mountains, surfing on the coast, or just taking it easy with a leisurely picnic in the park.

So prepare to experience Bilbao's outdoors by lacing up your hiking boots, grabbing your surfboard, or packing a picnic basket.

CHAPTER 6

BILBAO FOODS AND DRINKS

TRADITIONAL FOODS AND SPECIALTIES AT THEIR BEST

Bilbao is well-known for both its mouthwatering traditional cuisine and architectural wonders in addition to its rich cultural legacy. The focus on high-quality, fresh ingredients and the mastery of simple yet tasty cooking methods are hallmarks of Basque cuisine. Bilbao provides a wide variety of culinary pleasures, from substantial stews to delicious seafood. Here are some of Bilbao's top traditional foods and specialties to try:

1. Pintxos: Visiting Bilbao wouldn't be complete without indulging in some of the pintxos that are so well-known there. Pintxos are little bite-sized culinary concoctions that are served on a piece of bread and fastened with a toothpick, much like tapas. There are many different pintxos to select from, and the Basque Country is known

for its creative and delectable pintxos. The pintxo bars in Bilbao provide a culinary trip for your taste buds, with everything from classic pintxos like Gilda (a mix of olives, anchovies, and pickled peppers) to gourmet concoctions using regional delicacies like Iberian ham, fresh fish, and artisanal cheeses.

2. Codfish prepared in a Basque manner, or bacon a la Vizcaina, is a traditional dish that exemplifies Bilbao's culinary heritage. Salted cod is the main ingredient in this meal, which is prepared in a hearty tomato, pepper, onion, garlic, and olive oil sauce. Potatoes or a bed of sautéed veggies are often served with the fish. The flavorful sauce and the soft cod combine to provide a delicious meal that is a favorite among both residents and tourists.

3. Marmitako: The Basque Country's coastal districts are where this hearty fisherman's stew first appeared. Fresh tuna, potatoes, onions, peppers, tomatoes, and fish broth are the traditional ingredients used to make this warming meal. For the flavors to merge and

produce a beautifully thick and flavorful stew, the ingredients are cooked together. A warm and filling lunch is especially appealing in the colder months, and marmitako is the ideal embodiment of Bilbao's marine tradition.

4. Txangurro is a delicious crab dish that highlights Bilbao's plethora of seafood. A combination of crabmeat, breadcrumbs, onions, garlic, peppers, and spices is added to the crab shell to produce the meal. The crab is then filled, cooked till golden, and served immediately. Txangurro is a genuine treat for seafood enthusiasts due to the mix of soft crabmeat and savory filling. In Bilbao's seafood restaurants, it is often eaten as an appetizer or as a main meal.

5. Chuleta: A regional specialty and omnivore's pleasure, Archuleta is grilled beef prepared in the Basque way. A thick cut of quality beef, generally from a regional breed like Rubia Gallega or Buey de Marisma, is used in the meal. Salt is used to season the steak, which is then expertly grilled to produce a juicy, tasty piece of meat with a wonderful burnt exterior.

Chuleta is often served with grilled peppers, roasted potatoes, and a side of piquillo, a red pepper sauce in the Basque manner.

6. Idiazabal Cheese: This treasured handmade cheese comes from the Basque Country, and Bilbao is a great site to experience its genuine tastes. Idiazabal cheese, which is produced from raw milk from Latxa or Carranzana sheep, has a characteristic nutty and smoky taste that becomes better with age.

The cheese is often eaten on its own or with crusty bread, membrillo, or quince paste. It is popular among cheese lovers and commonly appears on cheese boards and in traditional Basque dishes because of its rich and nuanced tastes.

7. Goxua is a classic Basque delicacy that shouldn't be missed by people with a sweet craving. The layers of sponge cake, custard, and whipped cream in this decadent delicacy are covered in a layer of caramelized sugar. A delicious dessert that is creamy and decadent is

produced by the marriage of tastes and textures. Cherry is often placed on top of goxua as a garnish to enhance color and delicious taste. It is a well-liked option on dessert menus and at pastry shops in Bilbao.

8. Patxaran is a traditional liqueur from the Basque country that has a distinct position in Bilbao's culinary history. Patxaran, a liquor created by steeping sloe berries in anise-flavored vodka, has a distinctive ruby-red hue and tastes sweet and fruity with a tinge of spice.

It is often shipped as an aperitif over ice or as a digestif after a meal. The liquor epitomizes Basque customs and is the ideal way to cap off an unforgettable meal in Bilbao.

9. Talos: Also referred to as talk, talk is a kind of traditional Basque corn tortilla that is a mainstay of the local cuisine. Talos are made with a simple combination of cornmeal, water, and salt and are griddle-cooked until they have a golden crust. They are often eaten with a variety of fillings, such as roasted peppers, cheese, or

chorizo. Talos is an adaptable and filling snack that may be found at Bilbao's street markets and festivals.

10. Sidra: In Bilbao and the larger Basque Country, sidra, or Basque cider, is a popular libation. Basque cider, which is produced from apples from the area, has a distinctively sour and somewhat effervescent flavor.

Sidra is often served by pouring it from a height to aerate the cider, which improves its taste and produces an eye-catching show. Sidra homes, sometimes referred to as sagardotegia, are well-liked meeting spots where residents and guests may unwind with a crisp glass of cider and traditional Basque fare.

These are only a handful of the many traditional foods and delicacies available in Bilbao. A pleasure for the senses, discovering this bustling city's gastronomic offerings allows one to experience the rich cultural legacy and culinary prowess of the Basque people. Bilbao's traditional meals and specialties are certain to leave you with a profound appreciation for Basque cuisine and an outstanding dining experience, whether you're a food connoisseur or just want to taste the flavors of the area.

THE BEST DRINKS TO TRY

The great variety of drinks available in Bilbao reflects the city's dynamic environment and rich cultural past. Here are some of the greatest drinks to sample in Bilbao, ranging from deeply established Basque traditions to modern creations:

1. Txakoli: Bilbao is a great spot to experience this typical white wine from the Basque Country, which is a light and pleasant wine. Txakoli, a wine made from local grapes, has a sharp, acidic flavor and a somewhat sparkling appearance. To increase its effervescence, it is often poured into a glass from a height. Indulge in a glass of Txakoli while unwinding in a pintxos bar, or pair it with delectable seafood dishes for an unforgettable dining experience.

2. Kalimotxo: Kalimotxo is a well-known Basque cocktail produced by blending red wine with cola. It's a distinctive and delightful drink. Although it may seem strange, the flavorful red wine and the sweet cola combine to make a pleasantly tasty and well-balanced drink. Locals love Kalimotxo, particularly during celebrations and outdoor gatherings. It's the ideal option for a light drink while touring Bilbao.

3. Pacharán: For ages, Basques have sipped on pacharán, a traditional liquor. Pacharán, an alcoholic beverage with a rich crimson hue and a distinctive fusion of fruity and herbal aromas, is created by macerating sloe berries in anise-flavored vodka.

Pacharán, which is often served cold in tiny glasses, is frequently savored as a digestif or as a nightcap. It is a drink that you must sample while in Bilbao due to its unique flavor and cultural importance.

4. Sidra, sometimes referred to as basque cider, is a popular libation in Bilbao and the greater

Basque Country. Basque cider, which is produced with apples from the area, has a rich, reviving flavor that is tart and somewhat acidic.

Visit a sagardotegia, or traditional cider house, to get the whole Basque cider experience. To produce a natural effervescence, the cider is poured from a height in this special ceremony, which you may take part in. You may taste the essence of Basque cider culture via this unique experience.

5. Although the gin and tonic may not have come from Bilbao or the Basque Country, the city has embraced this traditional drink and given it its special spin. With various pubs and restaurants providing a large assortment of gins, tonics, and inventive garnishes, Bilbao has a booming gin and tonic scene.

Whatever your preference for a traditional G&T or want to experiment with cutting-edge gin mixes, Bilbao's gin and tonic culture will satiate your need for a well-made and revitalizing drink.

6. Craft Beer: With several regional breweries and beer bars springing up all over the city, craft beer has become more popular in Bilbao. If you like beer, don't forget to check out Bilbao's thriving craft beer industry. Discover the distinctive tastes and skills of Basque artisan brewers by tasting a selection of locally produced beers, from rich stouts to hoppy IPAs.

7. Coffee: Despite not strictly being a typical Basque beverage, coffee is crucial to Bilbao's everyday life. A thick cup of coffee may be enjoyed at any one of the city's many cafés and coffee shops, which are all part of its strong coffee culture.

The city of Bilbao has a wide selection of coffee alternatives to suit every taste, whether you want a robust espresso, a creamy cappuccino, or a silky café con leche. Spend a minute unwinding at one of the city's quaint cafés while savoring the scent and tastes of a fine cup of coffee.

8. Small beer glasses known as "burritos" are typical in Bilbao's pubs and taverns. It is

comparable to a little draft beer or a beer tester. With this beverage, you may try a variety of regional beers without committing to a full glass. It's a terrific chance to experience the vibrant ambiance of Bilbao's pubs while learning more about the regional beer culture and trying out new tastes.

9. Licor de Hierbas, often known as herb liqueur, is a typical digestif used in the Basque country. This fragrant liqueur delivers a distinctive combination of tastes that may vary from herbal and flowery to somewhat sweet and bitter. It is made by infusing a variety of herbs and spices in alcohol.

It is thought that serving Licor de Hierbas cold in tiny glasses would assist with digestion. It offers a pleasant and relaxing conclusion to a good lunch in Bilbao.

10. Basque Vermouth: In recent years, local manufacturers have created variations of the traditional fortified wine vermouth, which has gained popularity in Bilbao. Basque vermouth

often has a unique taste character since it is produced with a combination of regional herbs, spices, and botanicals. Basque vermouth is a lovely blend of bitter, sweet, and herbal aromas when served over ice with a slice of lemon or with traditional pintxos. It's a chic and refined option for an afternoon beverage or an aperitif.

A wide variety of fascinating drinks are available in Bilbao, reflecting both the Basque region's gastronomic legacy and the city's rich cultural past. The beverage culture in Bilbao has something to offer everyone, whether they like wine, craft beer, or exploring new traditional beverages. So raise a glass and toast to the tastes and adventures that this energetic and warm city has in store for you.

MODERN CUISINE TO TRY

Bilbao is renowned for both its booming contemporary gastronomy scene and its extensive culinary heritage. A lively gastronomic environment that mixes classic tastes with modern methods is the product of the city's embrace of innovation and originality in the culinary realm. You could try these trendy food alternatives when visiting Bilbao:

1. Molecular Gastronomy: Molecular gastronomy is a cutting-edge approach to cooking that emphasizes the creative and scientific manipulation of ingredients and preparation methods.

Restaurants that specialize in molecular gastronomy may be found in Bilbao, where they provide creative meals that push the frontiers of flavor, texture, and presentation. Spherification, foams, and liquid nitrogen are common ingredients used in these restaurants to provide distinctive and aesthetically beautiful culinary experiences.

2. Fusion food: Bilbao is a city of many ethnicities and influences, and this variety is reflected in the city's current cuisine. To generate intriguing and well-balanced taste combinations, fusion cuisine mixes ingredients from several culinary traditions. Restaurants in Bilbao

combine regional tastes with those from across the globe to create meals that are both recognizable and novel. These eateries provide a pleasant study of international cuisines, whether it be Basque-Asian fusion or Basque-Latin American fusion.

3. Farm-to-table: With an emphasis on locally produced, seasonally appropriate products, the farm-to-table movement has gained traction in Bilbao. Working closely with regional farmers, fishermen, and producers to source the freshest and best foods is a top priority for many contemporary restaurants in the city. These eateries often provide constantly changing menus that reflect the local harvest and the tastes of the moment. By eating at these places, you can discover Bilbao's authentic culinary scene while supporting regional farmers and sustainable methods.

4. Traditional pintxos and tapas are still regularly consumed in Bilbao, but many contemporary eateries have given these tiny dishes a creative makeover. Bilbao's chefs have improved the art

of tapas by using cutting-edge methods and unusual ingredients. With inventive tapas presentations and deconstructed pintxos, these eateries provide a novel spin on the traditional small plate experience. It's an opportunity to experience well-known tastes in novel and intriguing ways.

5. Seafood Reimagined: Bilbao is well known for its quantity of fresh seafood since it is a coastline city. Chefs have used this coveted resource in contemporary cooking in creative and surprising ways.

Restaurants that provide novel seafood meals may be found, such as seafood ceviche with unusual taste combinations, fish marinated in exotic spices, and seafood tartare with creative sides.

These meals showcase the sea's authentic tastes while also showcasing the culinary expertise of Bilbao's contemporary chefs.

6. Food that is vegetarian or vegan: The current culinary scene in Bilbao satisfies the rising

demand for vegetarian and vegan choices. You may discover restaurants that specialize in vegetarian and vegan food, with an emphasis on plant-based ingredients and inventive cooking methods.

These restaurants provide creative recipes that highlight the flavorful variety of plant-based ingredients, demonstrating that vegetarian and vegan cuisine can be interesting, filling, and full of gastronomic pleasures.

7. Modern cuisine in Bilbao includes sweets, where chefs may display their creative abilities and culinary mastery. Desserts made by pastry chefs are innovative and artistically spectacular, appealing to the mouth as well as the eye.

These masterpieces are a feast for the senses and the mind, ranging from delicate pastries with elaborate motifs to avant-garde dessert displays. Don't pass up the chance to enjoy these artistic food creations.

THE BEST CAFES AND RESTAURANTS IN BILBAO

A gastronomic wonderland, Bilbao offers a vast selection of eateries to suit every preference and price range. The city provides a diversified eating scene that accommodates all inclinations, from Michelin-starred restaurants to quiet cafés selling traditional pintxos. The following are a few of Bilbao's top eateries that you need to think about visiting:

1. Azurmendi: In the village of Larrabetzu, just outside of Bilbao, is where you'll find the three Michelin-star restaurants Azurmendi. This culinary jewel delivers a genuinely unique dining experience under the direction of renowned chef Eneko Atxa. Azurmendi is renowned for its inventive food, which uses products from the area and creative cooking methods. The wonderful gourmet trip is accompanied by breathtaking views from the restaurant, which is housed in a magnificent edifice surrounded by vineyards.

2. Nerua Guggenheim Bilbao is a Michelin-starred restaurant run by Chef Josean Alija, and it is housed within the famous

Guggenheim Museum. The idea of the restaurant emphasizes simplicity and purity while emphasizing the authentic tastes of locally sourced seasonal foods. Nerua provides a classy and polished eating experience that ideally complements a trip to the museum thanks to its clean and contemporary interior design.

3. Mina is a Michelin-starred establishment that honors Basque cuisine in a modern way. Innovative meals made by chef Alvaro Garrido are influenced by regional ingredients and tastes. A wonderful eating experience is created by the restaurant's attractive and contemporary decor and flawless service. For a gourmet tour through Basque Food, be sure to order from their tasting menu.

4. El Perro Chico is a well-known bistro-style eatery situated in Bilbao's Casco Viejo, the city's historic district. El Perro Chico is renowned for its inventive and contemporary Basque cuisine and provides a menu that emphasizes regional products and seasonal ingredients. A casual but memorable eating experience is made possible

by the restaurant's warm ambiance and helpful staff.

5. Café Irua: Located in the center of Bilbao, Café Irua is a renowned and storied café. This magnificent café, which was founded in 1903 and has maintained its vintage appeal, is a popular meeting spot for both residents and tourists.

Coffee, cocktails, and traditional Basque drinks like Kalimotxo are just a few of the beverages available at Café Irua, which is renowned for its elegant décor with high ceilings and stained glass windows. It's the ideal place to unwind, observe people, and take in the ambiance of the city.

6. La Via del Ensanche is a well-known pintxos pub in Bilbao that is well-known for its superb Basque tapas. This lively pub, which is located in the energetic Ensanche neighborhood, serves a variety of pintxos, including both classic favorites and cutting-edge variations.

The pub is a must-visit if you want to experience Bilbao's culinary culture in its entirety because of its vibrant atmosphere, welcoming staff, and delectable pintxos.

7. Café Boulevard: In Bilbao's Old Town, next to the Teatro Arriaga, lies a beautiful café called Café Boulevard. With timeless beauty, this historic café has been feeding residents and tourists since 1892.

Café Boulevard, which is well-known for its delicious coffee, pastries, and sandwiches, offers a warm and welcoming ambiance where visitors can unwind and take a wonderful break from seeing the city.

8. Gure Toki: Located in the Casco Viejo district, Gure Toki is a well-known pintxos restaurant. This busy restaurant is well known for its mouthwatering pintxos, which vary from traditional pairings to unique and inventive meals. The lively atmosphere and welcoming ambiance of the pub produce a genuine pintxos

experience that is popular with both residents and visitors.

9. Etxanobe: Known for its outstanding food, Etxanobe is a well-known restaurant in Bilbao that has been awarded a Michelin star. This beautiful institution provides expansive views of the city skyline and is situated on the top level of the Palacio Euskalduna.

Etxanobe, under the direction of chef Fernando Canales, creates outstanding meals by fusing traditional Basque tastes with cutting-edge cooking methods. The restaurant is a preferred option for a special fine dining experience because of its elegant setting, excellent service, and well-created dishes.

10. Since 1903, Bilbao has been served by the renowned local institution Café Nervión. This ancient café is a gathering place for people and a terrific place to experience the spirit of the city. It is situated in the busy Plaza Moya. Café Nervión, which is well-known for its authentic Basque pastries and cakes, is the ideal location

to enjoy a sweet treat with a cup of coffee or tea. Visitors are transported back in time by the café's nostalgic ambiance and antique appeal.

11. Eneko Bilbao: Located in the center of Bilbao, Eneko Bilbao is a restaurant operated by famous Basque chef Eneko Atxa. With a menu that emphasizes regional products and tastes, this restaurant offers a contemporary and lighthearted interpretation of Basque cuisine.

Eneko Bilbao is a great option for a calm but exceptional eating experience because of its warm ambiance. Try their specialties like the hake kokotxas or the Basque cheesecake; you won't regret it.

12. Bistrot La Ribera is a quaint eatery tucked away in the scenic Ribera Market, only steps from the river. This intimate restaurant emphasizes the use of seasonal, fresh products obtained from nearby vendors.

The menu offers a selection of meals made with a modern twist and influenced by Basque and Mediterranean cuisines. Bistrot La Ribera provides a pleasant dining experience in a distinctive setting with its rustic but contemporary design and kind service.

13. Zortziko: A Michelin star has been given to the famed Bilbao restaurant Zortziko. Under the direction of chef Daniel Garcia, Zortziko combines traditional Basque cooking methods with cutting-edge presentation. The menu offers a variety of elegant meals that highlight the best local products.

Zortziko is a great option for a special event or a memorable dining experience because of its stylish atmosphere and exceptional service.

14. In the center of the city sits the old café known as Café Iruna Bilbao. Since its founding in 1904, this famous business has maintained its vintage appeal. Café Iruna Bilbao, which is renowned for its exquisite architecture and gorgeous stained glass windows, provides a distinctive atmosphere to enjoy a cup of coffee or a cool beverage.

The café is the ideal location for a relaxing stop as you explore Bilbao since it also offers a variety of light snacks and pastries.

15. Featuring a blend of Basque and international tastes, Restaurante Mina is a Michelin-starred establishment. Chef Lvaro Garrido's culinary treasure provides a modern and unique eating experience. Innovative cuisine made with the freshest seasonal ingredients is featured on the menu.

Restaurante Mina offers a remarkable culinary trip in the center of Bilbao with its contemporary interior design and exceptional service.

These are just a handful of the numerous outstanding eateries and coffee shops Bilbao has to offer.

CHAPTER 7

BILBAO SHOPPING: THINGS YOU NEED TO KNOW

LOCAL ARTS AND CRAFTWORK

With its broad array of regional crafts and mementos, Bilbao, with its rich cultural past and creative traditions, is the ideal place to capture the spirit of the city and take home a piece of its distinctive personality. Here are some examples of the regional crafts and mementos one may get in Bilbao, ranging from traditional to modern designs:

1. Basque Berets: The "txapela," or Basque beret, is a well-known emblem of the area's cultural identity. Wool is used to make these flat, circular hats, which come in a variety of hues and designs. Traditional Basque berets are available at specialist hat stores all across Bilbao. The beret is not just a chic item, but also a significant keepsake that honors regional workmanship and tradition.

2. Bilbao and the Basque Country have a long history of producing textiles, so you may discover a wide variety of excellent linens and textiles there. These items, which range from handmade blankets and towels to tablecloths and napkins, exhibit elaborate patterns and workmanship. To find one-of-a-kind items that showcase the region's cultural heritage, look for shops and boutiques that specialize in Basque textiles.

3. Bilbao is home to skilled potters and ceramicists who produce exquisite handcrafted ceramics. Traditional Basque pottery often has vivid hues, complex designs, and themes drawn from nature and mythology. There are many ceramic products available, such as plates, bowls, vases, and ornamental tiles. These items make for lovely, useful keepsakes that bring a little regional creativity into your house.

4. Crafts made of wood: In Bilbao and the neighboring regions, woodworking is a thriving traditional craft. A variety of wooden products, including hand-carved furniture, ornamental

boxes, kitchenware, and figures, are made by skilled artists. Many of these items are handmade using traditional Basque techniques, making them one-of-a-kind and heartfelt gifts to bring back.

5. Bilbao's cuisine is well-known, and you may have a taste of it at home by buying Basque food items. There are many mouthwatering selections to choose from, including artisanal cheeses, olive oils, and preserves in addition to the well-known Basque sea salt known as "sal de Ana." To discover these genuine Basque goods in Bilbao, look for specialty food shops or markets. They make wonderful presents or pleasures for yourself.

6. Instruments of the Basque tradition: The Basque culture places a high value on music, and traditional instruments of the Basque tradition may be found. One such instrument is the "exist," a little wood flute-like instrument that is often used in traditional Basque celebrations. The "txalaparta" (a wooden percussion instrument) and the "ponderosa" (a kind of

tambourine) are two more instruments that are important in Basque music. Specialty stores carry these instruments, which are great keepsakes for music lovers.

7. Jewelry from the Basque Country: Basque jewelry displays the artistic talent of the area and integrates traditional designs and symbols. Look for jewelry with designs that honor the Basque cultural history and are crafted from materials like silver and natural gemstones. Jewelry made in the Basque region, which includes bracelets, rings, earrings, and pendants, provides a fashionable and meaningful way to remember your trip to Bilbao.

8. Bilbao is home to several artisanal chocolate establishments that create mouthwatering confections. These chocolates, which range from truffles to bonbons, are created using premium ingredients and often have distinctive tastes drawn from Basque customs and cuisine. Consuming these handcrafted chocolates is a celebration of Bilbao's culinary artistry as well as a pleasurable experience. These homemade

chocolates will please anybody who likes chocolate or is searching for a pleasant present.

9. Bilbao and the surrounding area are renowned for producing outstanding wines and ciders. Wine and cider tasting tours are a favorite pastime for aficionados, and you may purchase bottles of these libations to take home as a reminder of your trip to the Basque Country. There are several alternatives to pick from, ranging from deep and strong Rioja wines to crisp and refreshing Txakoli wines. Additionally, the distinctive and reviving taste profile of Basque ciders, or "sidra," is offered. Wine aficionados will love receiving these locally-made wines as presents or as great mementos.

10. Traditional Leather Goods: The leather industry is prospering in Bilbao, and the city is home to a wide selection of high-quality leather products. These products, which range from belts and accessories to purses and wallets, are well-made. For one-of-a-kind, long-lasting keepsakes that highlight the area's

leatherworking prowess, look for stores that specialize in leathercraft.

11. Bilbao is a center for modern art and design, and you can browse the city's galleries and shops to find one-of-a-kind works made by gifted creators. There are many modern art and design goods accessible, ranging from paintings and sculptures to home décor and clothing. Purchasing a work of local art or design enables you to not only support the creative industry but also infuse your house with a little of Bilbao's artistic flair.

12. Basque traditional instruments are important for maintaining this musical legacy since music is a major aspect of Basque culture. Look for specialist shops that sell traditional Basque instruments like the "alboka," a wind instrument fashioned from a horn and wooden pipes, or the "txalaparta," a wooden percussion instrument played with mallets. These distinctive instruments are not only lovely but also act as a reminder of the region's musical heritage and cultural customs.

13. Basque Handmade Shoes and Espadrilles: Bilbao is renowned for the quality of its shoemaking, and you can discover a selection of handcrafted shoes and espadrilles that combine age-old methods with cutting-edge styles. These footwear selections, which range from fashionable espadrilles to leather boots and sandals, demonstrate the area's commitment to both quality and elegance. You may enjoy the comfort and creativity that Bilbao is renowned for by buying a pair of handcrafted shoes or espadrilles.

14. Books & Literature in the Basque Language: The Basque language, Euskera, is an essential component of the local culture. Consider buying books or literature published in Euskera if you want to learn more about Basque history, literature, or language. Literature in the Basque language, including poetry, fiction, and non-fiction, is widely available in Bilbao's bookshops. These books not only provide fascinating insights into Basque culture, but they also make thoughtful and instructive gifts.

15. Locally produced handmade soaps and cosmetics are available in Bilbao from a variety of manufacturers that use natural ingredients and age-old techniques to create high-quality goods.

These regionally produced cosmetics, which range from handcrafted soaps and bath salts to lotions and creams, provide an opulent and environmentally friendly way to indulge yourself or make meaningful presents. To locate a variety of wonderful smells and skin care necessities, look for stores or markets that specialize in handmade beauty items.

You may immerse yourself in Bilbao's lively culture and bring a piece of its history home by perusing the local crafts and mementos. Whether you choose a conventional

POPULAR SHOPPING AREAS

In Bilbao, a vibrant city, there are several shopping malls where tourists may indulge in retail therapy and learn about well-known national and worldwide companies. Here are a few of Bilbao's most well-known retail areas:

1. Centro Comercial Zubiarte is a contemporary retail complex that has a broad selection of local and foreign fashion brands, such as Zara, H&M, and Mango. It is situated in the affluent area of Indautxu. Zubiarte offers a delightful shopping experience with its modern architecture and open layout. Along with a variety of eateries and cafés, the complex also has a movie theater.

2. Gran Via: Bilbao's major retail district is dotted with a wide variety of shops and boutiques. It extends from the city's center to the Abando district and has a variety of high-end designer labels, department stores, and neighborhood merchants. Shoppers may get everything they need here, including technology, household goods, and apparel and accessories. Gran Via is a dynamic and busy retail district that accommodates a range of preferences and price points.

3. One of the biggest shopping facilities in the Bilbao metropolitan region is Centro Commercial Ballonti, which is located in the neighboring town of Portugalete. It has a wide

variety of retailers, including ones for clothing, cosmetics, electronics, and home furnishings. Ballonti provides a nice atmosphere and excellent river views thanks to its waterfront setting. The retail mall also has a multiplex theater and several restaurants.

4. Bilbondo: Another well-liked retail complex, Bilbondo is situated in the municipality of Sondika not far from Bilbao. It provides a variety of renowned brands, budget retailers, and niche shops. The enormous hypermarket in Bilbondo, where customers can get food, home goods, and other stuff, is well recognized. The retail mall has plenty of parking and is close to a public transit hub.

5. One of the biggest shopping malls in northern Spain is called Max Center, and it is located in the town of Barakaldo. It offers a wide range of clothing, accessories, technology, and furniture for the house. Major worldwide companies like Primark, Decathlon, and Media Markt can be found at Max Center, along with a variety of dining establishments such as restaurants and

fast food joints. In addition to having entertainment options, the mall is a well-liked spot for both shopping and leisure pursuits.

6. The Vialia Estación de Bilbao retail center is situated within the major railway station of Bilbao and provides a distinctive shopping experience. There are many different retailers at the mall, including specialized, fashion, and accessory shops. The Bilbao Vialia Estación is renowned for its elegant architecture, which combines contemporary style with the old-world elegance of the railway station. Additionally, it organizes exhibits and cultural activities all year round.

7. Artea: A sizable retail complex that serves a wide variety of consumers is located in the municipality of Leioa, not far from Bilbao. It contains a variety of foreign fashion labels, home furnishings shops, and entertainment venues. In addition, Artea has a food court where guests may sample a variety of dishes. Families often visit this retail mall because of its roomy layout and wealth of attractions.

These are just a handful of the well-known retail malls in and around Bilbao. These centers provide a variety of alternatives to fit various interests and budgets, whether you're seeking fashion, technology, home items, or leisure activities.

CHAPTER 8

NIGHTLIFE IN BILBAO

The thriving city of Bilbao has a diverse and fascinating nightlife scene. For anybody wishing to enjoy the city after dark, Bilbao has lots to offer, from hip pubs and nightclubs to live music venues and cultural activities. Here is a deeper look into Bilbao's nightlife and some of the best destinations to check out:

1. Casco Viejo: Also referred to as the Old Town, Casco Viejo is a vibrant and evocative district that comes to life at night. Numerous taverns and pintxo (Basque tapas) restaurants like its winding lanes, generating a lively environment. In Casco Viejo, you may find both modern cocktail bars and conventional Basque pubs. The best way to experience the evening in this region is to visit many bars, sample various pintxos, and take in the vibrant atmosphere.

2. Muelle de Marzana is a chic neighborhood along the river that has become well-known for

its nightlife. This once-industrial area is now home to a variety of hip bars, pubs, and clubs that provide something for every taste. Everything from calm cafés to vivacious nightclubs performing a variety of musical genres may be found here. A variety of local and foreign venues can be found in Muelle de Marzana, offering varied nightlife.

3. Plaza Nueva: Casco Viejo's main area, Plaza Nueva, is a hive of activity day and night. The area is surrounded by a large number of pubs and cafés, making it the perfect place to relax with a drink or two and take in the bustling ambiance. The weekend nightlife scene is energized by the live music concerts and street activities that often take place in the area. A terrific place to start for a night out in Bilbao, Plaza Nueva is a well-liked gathering spot for residents and tourists alike.

4. Another district in Bilbao that provides a lively nightlife scene is Indautxu. There are several taverns, pubs, and clubs there that may accommodate all tastes and preferences.

Indautxu offers alternatives to fit every mood, whether you're looking to unwind in a craft beer pub or have a wild night out dancing. The location draws a broad clientele, ranging from youthful partygoers to older professionals, which promotes a fun and welcoming environment.

5. Bilbao La Vieja: Bilbao La Vieja, a neighborhood, has recently undergone redevelopment and has become a hip and creative region. It is the location of an increasing number of trendy clubs, cutting-edge cocktail lounges, and cultural venues. A youthful, artistic community is drawn to the area because they value its unconventional and alternative vibe. If you want to check out the city's unique and creative nightlife, Bilbao La Vieja is a great option.

6. Live Music Venues: Bilbao has a thriving live music scene, with both local and foreign performers performing at several venues. Rock, jazz, indie, and electronic music events often take place at locations such as Kafe Antzokia, Santana 27, and Stage Live. These places are

fantastic places to listen to live music and take in the vigor and excitement of Bilbao's music culture.

7. Bilbao's nightlife extends beyond pubs and clubs; the city also provides distinctive cultural activities after hours. For instance, the Guggenheim Museum often provides nighttime activities including art exhibits, movie screenings, and performances.

Additionally, Bilbao's theaters and cultural institutions often arrange evening entertainment, including stand-up comedy, dance performances, and theatrical plays. Through these cultural encounters, tourists may get a new perspective on the city's nightlife and become fully immersed in Bilbao's creative and intellectual environment.

8. The gourmet scene in Bilbao is another chance to experience the city's culinary wonders at night. Many eateries and pintxo bars stay up later in the evening, giving patrons the option to engage in gastronomic exploration. Bilbao offers

a variety of foods to suit your taste, whether you're in the mood for inventive fusion dishes or classic Basque fare. A Bilbao-only spectacular dining experience is created by the marriage of delectable cuisine, superb wine, and a vibrant atmosphere.

9. Rooftop Bars and Terraces: Bilbao has several rooftop bars and terraces that provide breathtaking views of the city skyline for those wanting a more elevated experience. These lofty locations provide a chic backdrop for sipping a martini while admiring expansive views of the city and its surroundings.

Rooftop bars in Bilbao provide an unforgettable way to experience the city's nightlife, whether you're seeking a romantic evening or a casual get-together with friends.

10. Festivals & Events: Bilbao is renowned for its vivacious festival culture, and several of these events go on far into the night. The city holds several music festivals, cultural events, and street festivities all year round. The Bilbao BBK

Live music festival, one of the most well-known events, draws well-known worldwide performers and music fans from all over the globe. With music, dancing, and celebrations that go well into the night, these festivals provide an exhilarating environment.

11. Casino Bilbao: For those seeking some fun and excitement, Casino Bilbao provides a glitzy and exhilarating nightlife experience. The casino, which is in the center of the city, offers a variety of games, including roulette, blackjack, and poker. A spectacular evening out is guaranteed for those seeking a little glitz thanks to the casino's additional programming, which includes live music performances, special events, and a range of culinary choices.

12. Late-Night Shopping: Bilbao has a few late-night shopping options if you're a night bird who appreciates shopping. You may indulge in retail therapy long after the sun sets at El Corte Inglés, one of Spain's major department shops that are open till late. For those who love to shop at night, certain boutiques and businesses in

well-known districts like Gran Via and Casco Viejo extend their hours, offering a distinctive shopping experience.

The nightlife in Bilbao provides a wide variety of experiences, from buzzing pubs and clubs to cultural activities and culinary explorations. Bilbao has plenty to offer everyone's tastes, whether you want to dance the night away, take in the city's art and music culture, or just enjoy a relaxing evening of food and entertainment. With its lively and welcoming environment, the city makes sure that tourists can make the most of their evenings in Bilbao and create priceless memories.

THINGS TO AVOID WHEN TRAVELING TO BILBAO

To guarantee a comfortable and pleasurable trip to Bilbao, it's vital to be aware of several things to avoid. To remember, have the following in mind:

1. Pickpocketing and Theft: As with any well-known tourist location, pickpocketing and

theft must be avoided at all costs. In crowded places, stay away from carrying valuables or big amounts of cash. Be careful where you put your things and be aware of your surroundings, particularly in crowded tourist locations, on public transit, and at well-known sights. To protect your belongings, think about utilizing a money belt or a safe bag.

2. Unlicensed Taxis: It is advised to only use licensed taxis in Bilbao to prevent fraud and overcharging. Identification and a meter are prominently visible in official taxis. Avoid using "pirate taxis," or unregistered taxis, since they may overcharge or exploit visitors. It's best to utilize trusted taxi services, reserve cabs using dependable applications, or use hotel services.

3. Drinking excessively: Bilbao has a thriving nightlife with many pubs and clubs, but it's crucial to drink with caution. Drinking too much may make you more vulnerable, affect your judgment, and put you in danger. To guarantee your safety, be aware of your limitations, drink

enough water, and always have a plan for transportation or other arrangements.

4. Scams and Street sellers: Be wary of street sellers who can attempt to offer you fakes or inferior items. When contacted by strangers asking for personal information or proposing dubious bargains, proceed with caution. Avoid participating in street games or gambling frauds since they might result in financial losses or victimization.

5. Protests & Demonstrations: Like many cities, Bilbao sometimes sees protests or demonstrations. Although these activities are usually calm, it is best to stay away from crowded locations and places where protests are taking place to protect your safety. Follow the instructions of local authorities on any current protests and keep up with local news.

6. Unfamiliar Districts at Night: Despite Bilbao's reputation as a safe city, it is nevertheless advisable to use care, particularly at night while traveling through unknown districts. When

going after dark, stay in well-lit, busy locations, and think about utilizing a reliable cab service or public transit. Always err on the side of caution if you have any doubts about a location's safety.

7. Cultural sensitivity: It's crucial to respect the local traditions, customs, and culture while traveling to any place. When visiting places of worship or more conservative locations, be conscious of acceptable attire guidelines. Learn the fundamental greetings and traditions of the area to respect the people who live there. Avoid talking about delicate subjects that might be seen as impolite or insulting.

8. Over-traveled Locations: Particularly during the busiest travel times of the year, certain well-liked tourist destinations may become overcrowded. While it's wonderful to see famous locations, be ready for crowds and long lines. To have a more genuine and pleasurable experience, think about visiting renowned sights at off-peak hours or exploring lesser-known locations.

You may improve your safety, prevent possible fraud, and have a more enjoyable trip in Bilbao by keeping these things in mind. Keep in mind to always use common sense, keep educated, and show respect for local traditions. Have fun traveling to Bilbao!

In conclusion, Bilbao is a fascinating city that provides a wide range of experiences for all kinds of tourists. Bilbao has it all, whether you're attracted to it for its extensive history, cutting-edge buildings, exciting nightlife, or mouthwatering food. This city expertly combines innovation and history to create a distinctive ambiance that is both warm and fascinating.

Everyone who visits Bilbao is left with a positive impression, whether they spend time at the Guggenheim Museum or wander along the charming riverbank. For everyone looking for an engaging vacation experience, it is a must-visit location because of its lovely streets, friendly residents, and cultural riches.

I hope that after you finish reading this book, you'll be motivated and prepared to go on your Bilbao adventure. This guide has given you insightful information, useful advice, and alluring suggestions whether you're organizing a quick holiday or a prolonged stay.

Pack your luggage, explore Bilbao's enchantment, and let this extraordinary city mesmerize your senses. Allow it to create a lasting impression on your vacation memories with its distinctive mix of history, art, food, and bright energy. When you arrive, Bilbao will welcome you with open arms and be happy to show you around. Happy travels!

Printed in Great Britain
by Amazon